DIVINITY & HUMANITY, ONE SINGLE ENTITY

as per the Bible, Saints, Other Religions & Notables!

Joseph Kerba, B.Ph.Ph.Ch.

Holzer Books LLC

Published 2024

Printed in the United States of America

First Edition
ISBN (print): 978-1-963380-23-1
ISBN (e-book): 978-1-963380-24-8

For information, address:
Holzer Books LLC 8 The Green, Ste. A
Dover, Delaware 19901 USA

For information about special discounts available for bulk purchases, sales promotions, and educational needs, contact:
info@holzerbooksllc.com
+1 (888) 901-7776

Contents

TO THE HOLY SPIRIT

INTRODUCTION

This book is based on a premise, among others, stated in _1 Corinthians 6:19_, as follows:

'Do you not know that your bodies are temples of the Holy Spirit, who is in you, whom you have received from God?'

Accordingly, every one of us is _'body + Holy Spirit'_, two entities in one, belonging to God, as per verse 20 of 1 Corinthians Chapter 6:

'For ye are bought with a price: therefore glorify God in your body, and in your spirit, which are God's.'

Athanasius, Bishop of Alexandria, Egypt, stated clearly what the title of this book declares:

'God became man so that man could become God.'

Now, Jesus Christ is _God & man_, _Holy Spirit & body_, two in one, belonging to God...

Well, Jesus is God, an integral part of the Holy Trinity, with God the Father and the Holy Spirit; one could therefore conclude that having our _'bodies,'_ as _'temples'_ of the _'Holy Spirit'_ makes us _'humans,'_ with *'God within each and every one of us*,' as a *'Divine Sparkle':* '*a true communion of God and man.'*

In concluding that we are all *'human & divine*,' I am *in no way demeaning God*, but rather *dignifying humans*, thereby *underscoring the enormous value of Who is in us*, all through our lives: *we are not only 'mortal flesh*,' but *having an 'immortal soul'* that is *'inseparable of our bodies until the instant of our death.'* Then, *this 'Divine Sparkle' returns to 'Its Source, the Holy Spirit,' freely roaming the 'universe'* in what we refer to as *'Heaven, Paradise or the Celestial Kingdom'*; those references *do not point to a 'specific location up there,' 'unattainable to living humans*,' but to '*the whole*' of a *'refreshed universe' among the living and the dead of 'all generations, past, present and future*,' the dead having been transformed into *'saintly angels*,' surrounding the living, helping them to become in turn eventual *'angel-saints*,' upon their *'new birth' at the moment of their 'death.'*

Christ Himself referred to us as 'angels' in Matthew 22:30,

'At the resurrection people will neither marry nor be given in marriage; they will be like the angels in heaven.'

I have written a book, titled: *'OUR SOUL IS GOD: From Him and to Him'* (*ISBN : 978-2-414-13501-1*); a number of quotations from that book are reproduced in this one.

4

1

THE HOLY SPIRIT IN DIFFERENT RELIGIONS.

CHRISTIAN:

- *Ecclesiastes 12:7,*

  'Then shall the *dust* [out of which God made man's body] *return to the earth* as it was: and *the spirit shall return unto God who gave it.*'

- *Genesis 2:7,*

  'Then the Lord God formed a man from the dust of the ground and *breathed into his nostrils the breath of life, and the man became a living being.*'

- *Luke 17:20-21,*

  'Once, on being asked by the Pharisees when the kingdom of God would come, Jesus replied, "The coming of the kingdom of God is not something that can be observed, nor will people say, 'Here it is,' or 'There it is,' because *the kingdom of God is in your midst.*'

- *1 Corinthian 6:19,*

   'Do you not know that *your bodies are temples of the Holy Spirit, who is in you*, whom you have received from God? You are not your own.'

- *1 Corinthians 6:17,*

   'He who is *joined to the Lord becomes one spirit with him.*'

- *Matthew 16:26,*

   'What good will it be for someone to gain the whole world, yet forfeit their *soul*?'

HINDUISM :

- *Swami Bhaskarananda,*

   '*A spiritually illuminated soul lives in the world*, yet is *never contaminated by it.*'

- *Bhavard Gitâ (Yoga),*

   'The Vedas teach that *the soul is divine, only held in the bondage of matter; perfection will be reached when this bond will burst*; and the word they use for it is, therefore, Mukti —*freedom from the bonds of imperfection, freedom from death and misery.'*

• <u>Swami Vivekanada,</u>

'The body is mortal, but <u>the person dwelling in the body is immortal and immeasurable.</u>'

'You are incarnations of God, all of you. You are incarnations of the Almighty, Omnipresent, Divine Principle. You may laugh at me now, but the time will come when you will understand. You must. *Nobody will be left behind.*

The awakening of the soul to its bondage and its effort to stand up and assert itself - this is called life.

There is no other teacher but your own soul.

There is only one Soul in the Universe. There is no 'you' or 'me'; all variety is merged into the absolute unity, the one infinite existence - God.

Soul, Unity, Infinite.

<u>*The soul is neither born, nor does it ever die*</u>; nor having once existed, does it ever cease to be. The <u>*soul is without birth, eternal, immortal, and ageless*</u>. It is not destroyed when the body is destroyed.

We can think of our material body as the field and our *immortal soul* as the *knower* of the field.

The impermanent has no reality; *reality lies in the eternal*. Those who have seen the boundary between these two have attained the end of all knowledge. Realize that which pervades the universe is *indestructible*; no power can affect this unchanging, imperishable reality.

The Kingdom of heaven is in you, *God is in you*. *He is the Soul of our souls. See Him in your own soul.*

In one word, the ideal is that *you are Divine*.

The problem is that we are attached to our body while *it is the Spirit that is truly immortal*.

The total sum of all the cells of an organism is a person. Accordingly, *each soul is like a cell* and *the aggregate of all cells is God.*

If I, as an Oriental have to worship *Jesus of Nazareth*, there is only one way, that is, to *worship him as God* and nothing else.

Spirituality is the science of the soul.

Serving others is serving God.

The body is but an instrument of the Spirit. Whatever the Spirit dictates, the body has to agree.

The Buddha and the Christ are symbols for two spiritual offices that are meant to guide the evolutions of earth. The Buddha is the one who sits on top of the Sea of Samsara and holds the balance. The Christ is the one who descends into that Sea of Samsara, to those who are lost in ignorance.

The Self when it appears behind the universe is called *God. The same Self when it appears behind this little universe—the body—is the soul*.

You have to *grow from the inside out*. None can teach you, none can make you spiritual.

There is no other teacher but your own soul.

I am a *Hindu*, I am proud to belong to a religion which has taught the world both tolerance and universal acceptance. We believe not only in universal toleration, but *we accept all religions as true.*'

ISLAM :

* *Sourah Maryam, Quran 19: 15-21 – (Shia),*

'And peace be upon him the day he was born, and the day he dies, and the *Day he is raised alive.*

9

And mention in the Scripture Mary, when she withdrew from her people to an eastern location.

She screened herself away from them, and *We sent to her Our spirit*, and He appeared to her as an *immaculate human*.

She said, "I take refuge from you in the Most Merciful, should you be righteous."

He said, "I am only the *messenger of your Lord*, *to give you the gift of a pure son*."

She said, "*How can I have a son, when no man has touched me, and I was never unchaste?*"

He said, "*Thus said your Lord*, 'It is easy for Me, and We will make him a sign for humanity, and *a mercy from Us*. It is a matter already decided.'"'

- *Averros Ibn-Rushd* (*Sunni*),

'The Material Intellect is single, *linked to* an *immortal substance* different from the human body, and is shared and commonly used by all humans. The uniqueness of the material intellect assures the unity of the Universals, *the immortal substance assures its immortality.*

The *human soul emanates from the unique universal soul united.*'

- Jalal Al-Din Rûmi (Sufi),

'Do you know what you are?
You are a *manuscript of a divine letter.*

You are a mirror reflecting a noble face.
This universe is not outside of you.
<u>*Look inside yourself*</u>;
everything that you want, you are already that.

<u>*Soul*</u>, if you want to learn secrets,
your heart must forget about
shame and dignity.
<u>*You are God's lover*</u>.
yet you worry
what people are saying.

There is a <u>*community of the spirit*</u>.

I belong to no religion. <u>*My religion is love*</u>. Every heart is my temple.

<u>*Soul of all souls*</u>, life of all life—you are <u>*That*</u>.
<u>*When you do things from your soul*</u>, you feel a river of joy within you.

You are not a drop in a ocean
<u>*You are entire ocean in a drop*</u>.

<u>*The soul of the Universe*</u> awaits to enfold you in pure white light.

You are more valuable than both
heaven and earth. What else can I say?

You don't know your own worth.
Do not sell yourself at a ridiculous price,
You who are so valuable in God's eyes.

When you look for *God*,
God is in the look of your eyes
In the thought of looking,
nearer to you than your self,
or things that have happened to you.

Death has nothing to do with going away.
The sun sets.
The moon sets.
But they are not gone.

You mustn't be afraid of death,
you're a *deathless soul*
you can't be kept in a dark grave
you're filled with God's glow.
be happy with your beloved
you can't find any better
the world will shimmer
because of *the diamond you hold*.

My soul is from elsewhere, I'm sure of that, and
I intend to end up there.

The Inspiration You Seek
Is *Already Within You*.

Be Silent And Listen.

Whenever you are alone, remind yourself that God has sent everyone else away so that there is only *you and Him*.

What you are seeking is also seeking you.'

2

THE HOLY SPIRIT, REFERENCED BY SAINTS/NOTABLES.

- *<u>Saint John of the Cross</u>:*

'Oh, then, <u>*soul*</u>... so anxious to know the dwelling *place of your Beloved that you may go in quest of <u>Him</u> and be united with Him*, now we are telling you that *<u>you yourself are His dwelling and His secret chamber and hiding place</u>*... so close to you as to be *<u>within you</u>*... What more do you want, <u>*O soul*</u>! And what else do you search for outside, when *<u>within yourself you possess</u>... your Beloved whom you desire and seek?*... There is but one difficulty, *even though He does <u>abide within you</u>, He is hidden.*

<u>God sustains every soul and dwells in it substantially, even though it be that of the greatest sinner in the world</u>, and this union is natural.'

- *Saint Vincent-de-Paul:*

'*I ask Our Lord to be the Spirit of your spirit* and the strength of your arm in order to destroy ignorance and sin, two monsters in God's Church.'

- *Socrates:*

'*The end of life is to be like unto God*; and *the soul following God, will be like unto Him*; *He being the beginning, middle, and end of all things.*'

- *Cicero:*

'If I err in my belief that the *souls of men are immortal*, I err gladly, and do not wish to lose so delightful an error.

This is the truth: *as from a fire aflame thousands of sparks come forth*, even so *from the Creator an infinity of beings have life and to him return again.*

One who sees *the Supersoul accompanying the individual soul in all bodies* and who understands that *neither the soul nor the Supersoul is ever destroyed*, actually sees.'

- *Victor Hugo*:

'I am a soul. I know well that <u>what I shall render up to the grave is not myself. That which is myself will go elsewhere. Earth, thou art not my abyss!</u>'

- *Gibran Khalil Gibran*:

  'I existed from all eternity and, behold, I am here; and I shall exist till the end of time, for my being has no end.'

- *Eckhart von Hochheim*:

  'God is in all things, but so far as God is Divine and so far as He is rational, God is nowhere so properly as in the soul - in the innermost of the soul.'

- *Epictetus*:

  'You are a little soul carrying about a corpse.'

- *Saint Teresa of Avila*:

  'Each of us has a soul, but we forget to value it. We don't remember that *we are creatures made in the image of God. We don't understand the great secrets hidden inside of us.'*

- *Léo Tolstoy*:

  'Love is life. All, everything that I understand, I understand only because I love. Everything is, everything exists, only because I love. Everything is united by it alone. *Love is God, and to die means that I, a particle of love, shall return to the general and eternal source.'*

- *Saint John Bosco*:

  'God found a way *to nourish our souls* in a convenient spiritual manner : *He gave them His Own Divinity.*'

- *Albert Einstein :*

  'Coincidences is God's way of remaining anonymous.'

3

OUR SOUL IS GOD, FROM HIM & TO HIM, DIVINITY & IMMORTALITY.

OUR SPIRIT IS OUR SOUL, FUNDAMENTALLY THE SAME!

Dear readers,

You could have been surprised or even shocked by the title of my book and that of this chapter; please accept my apology! Those titles are sourced from a _personal inspiration from the Holy Spirit_, duly confirmed by indisputable facts, presented in the first two chapters of this book; please allow me to underscore some of them, as follows:

- _Ecclesiastes 12:7,_

    'Then shall the dust [out of which God made man's body] return to the earth as it was, and _the spirit shall return to God Who gave it.'_

- *Genesis 2:7,*

'Then the Lord God formed a man from the dust of the ground and *breathed into his nostrils the breath of life, and the man became a living being.*'

- *1 Corinthian 6:19,*

'Do you not know that *your bodies are temples of the Holy Spirit, who is in you*, whom you have received from God? You are not your own.'

- *1 Corinthians 6:17,*

'He who is *joined to the Lord becomes one spirit with him.*'

- *Sanatana Dharma and Yoga,*

'The Vedas teach that *the soul is divine, only held in the bondage of matter; perfection will be reached when this bond will burst*; and the word they use for it is, therefore, Mukti — *freedom from the bonds of imperfection, freedom from death and misery.*'

- *Bhavard Gitâ (Yoga),*

'The body is mortal, but the person dwelling in the body is immortal and immeasurable.'

- *Swami Vivekanada,*

'There is only one Soul in the Universe. There is no 'you' or 'me'; all variety is merged into the absolute unity, the one infinite existence - God.

The soul is neither born, nor does it ever die; nor having once existed, does it ever cease to be. *The soul is without birth, eternal, immortal, and ageless. It is not destroyed when the body is destroyed.*

The Kingdom of heaven is in you, *God is in you. He is the Soul of our souls. See Him in your own soul.*

In one word, the ideal is that *you are Divine.*

The total sum of all the cells of an organism is a person. Accordingly, *each soul is like a cell and the aggregate of all cells is God*.

The Self when it appears behind the universe is called God. The same Self when it appears behind this *little universe—the body—is the soul.'*

- *Averros Ibn-Rushd (Sunni),*

'*Soul of all souls*, life of all life—you are That.'

'*You mustn't be afraid of death*, you're a *deathless soul*

you can't be kept in a dark grave
you're filled with God's glow.
be happy with your beloved
you can't find any better
the world will shimmer
because of *the diamond you hold.*

My soul is from elsewhere, I'm sure of that, and
I intend to end up there.'

With the above attributes in mind, allow me to present to you the *blurb*, on the back cover of my book, titled: '*OUR SOUL IS GOD, From Him and to Him*,' as follows:

'This book is an attempt to counter the *mystery* of the soul; the definition of *a mystery is a religious truth that one can know only by revelation and cannot fully understand.*

I have been inspired that *every one of our souls is in fact God Almighty, residing in us, as of our conception and until our death*. My inspiration is based on *multiple quotations from the Holy Books, both Christian and non-Christian, as well as from notables* such as Gandhi, Martin Luther King Jr., Nelson Mandela and Gibran Khalil Gibran, among many others. *By demystifying our souls, the Holy Trinity, heaven, purgatory, hell, mercy, divinity, immortality, bilocation, near-death experiences* and our passage through our mothers' wombs are demonstrated by plausible explanations that *shed a new light to human understanding.*'

Conclusion:

You do not have to take my word about the _'mystery' of our souls_; please refer to _quotations from the Bible, from Saints and texts from other religions and from revered thinkers_, all of which echo my inspiration in a very clear and precise manner.

I also wish to _clarify a second distinction in our faith_ that seems to refer to a _'dichotomy' of spirit and soul;_ for me, _they are one and the same_, and should be considered as such, despite certain verses and teachings that treat them differently, rather than interchangeably. In fact, _Vatican II_ confirms the following: _'The human person, though made of body and soul, is a unity. In itself, in its very bodily condition, it synthesizes the elements of the material world, which through it are thus brought to their highest perfection.'_ Moreover, the Church teaches that _'the soul signifies the spiritual 'principle' of man... The human body is human, precisely because it is animated by a spiritual soul.' (Catechism of the Catholic Church 363-364)_

4

GOD'S EXISTENCE.

Is God's existence debatable? Well, yes! Atheists deserve an answer that is not only related to *blind faith* or to *biblical references* that could rightfully be questioned.

On the other hand, yet another question pops up: are certain *religious beliefs* that have been based on *blind faith* for years, *incompatible with evolving Sciences*? The answer is *no*.

Firstly, a number of *Church teachings* have been either *dropped or recalibrated* in an *evolution of our faith, guided by the Holy Spirit*. Others will certainly follow, as prophesized in this book.

For example, *Limbo*: this was a recognized Middle Ages *Catholic theology* that applied to all who *died before Christ*, and therefore were *not baptised*, and also to *babies* who similarly died before having such an opportunity. All were to head to a *border place between heaven and hell where they were not condemned to punishment, but were nonetheless deprived of eternal happiness with God* in heaven. The Limbo theology was dropped relatively recently, in *2007*, on the basis of God's mercy and Christ's call in *Matthew 19:14*, as follows:

'Let the little children come to me, and do not hinder them, for the kingdom of heaven belongs to such as these.'

Another example of dropped beliefs is that of *Galileo*; in *1616*, the *Inquisition* declared him to be *formally heretical.* His book was banned and he was sentenced to die; following his forced rebuttal of his beliefs, the death penalty was changed to a light regimen of penance and imprisonment; he was then held in a *villa arrest for the rest of his life. He died in 1642.*

Pope Jean-Paul II, on October 31, 1992, formally apologized to Galileo, in the first of many famous apologies, on behalf of the Church, during his papacy.

Pope Joseph Ratzinger did the same, while repeatedly insisting on the *mathematical structure of the universe*; this structure will be discussed later at length in this chapter. In the meantime, please note the Pope's reference to *mathematics and Galileo*, on *January 9, 2008* : 'The *great Galileo* said that *God* wrote the book of nature in the form of *the language of mathematics.* My readers are cordially invited to read further on : *www.chiesa.espressonline.it*; 'Faith By Numbers. When Ratzinger Puts on Galileo's Robes!'

Let us turn again to Pope Ratzinger on yet another subject, dealing with *Science and Faith*, that puts a dent in the Church's prior condemnation of *Darwin's creation theories* that seemed to *oppose* the *biblical expressions in the Old Testament*. There again, Ratzinger said that his predecessors – *Pope John Paul II and Pope Pius XII* had indicated that '*there is no opposition between the religious theory of faith and the evidence of the empirical science.*' This topic on *Adam & Eve* and the *Original Sin*, as contrasted with Darwin's *evolutionary theories* will be addressed in detail in *Chapter 8* of this book.

In the meantime, the pontiff's following quotation, referring to Pope John Paul II's statement is a *revelation* of sorts; it sheds a lot of light on the relationship between faith and science: '*scientific truth*, which is itself a form of *participation in the divine truth*, can help philosophy and theology to understand better the human person and the sacred revelation to the man, *revealed and perfectly complemented by Jesus Christ.*'

Lastly, in reference to Pope Ratzinger, in his audience was also present the late *Stephen Hawking, the theoretician of 'The Origin of the Universe,' and author of the best-seller 'Brief History of Time.'* In an interview which the late Mr. Hawking had granted to the Reuter's agency, he said: '*It is not religious in the normal meaning of the word. I think the universe is governed by the laws of science. It may be that these laws have been commanded by God, but God does not act to violate them!*'

Back to *Science and mathematics,* in the quest to ascertain whether *God exists* or that all creation, having no Creator or beginning, just happened to *appear out of thin air*:

Well, in *1931, Einstein* visited the Mt. Wilson Observatory in Los Angeles to examine the evidence presented in *1929* by the *astronomer Edwin Hubble*, concluding that *galaxies were expanding outward*, which meant that they had been much closer together in the past. Einstein, after peering through the telescope, examined the evidence and then concluded: '*I now see the necessity of a beginning!*'

Decades later, in *1965,* two U.S. scientists detected the remnants of the *initial burst of energy: the 'Big Bang';* this was a moment, *13.8 billion years ago,* when the *universe began* as a *tiny dense fireball that exploded.* Accordingly, as per scientists, the universe began with every speck of its energy jammed into a very tiny point that exploded with an incredible force, *creating matter* and pro-pelling it *outward* to make *billions of galaxies* and *create energy, space and time.* This theory was *inspired by* the discovery of the *expanded universe by Edwin Hubble.* It was *first proposed in* 1927 by a *Roman Catholic priest and physicist George Lemaître;* you may be informed further on the *Big Bang* topic in *wikipedia.org,* as well as from the *BBC series 'Universe,'* among other references.

Now, could the Big Bang theory reflect what is referred to in *Genesis 1:1,* as follows: '*In the beginning, God created the heavens and the earth?'* Would that also mean that *matter and energy* could have appeared at a certain *point in time* through a *Supreme Creator* who *existed beforehand?* Let us dig deeper into that possibility, seeking to identify the complexities and extreme accuracies of what could be described as *miraculous* in nature, in that *no human intelligence* could entail by *its immediacy!*

Well, first and foremost: in *1973,* cosmologist *Brandon Carter* con-firmed that *the independent constants or laws in physics* have one highly unusual characteristic in common, in that they are *precisely the values needed to establish and sustain a universe, carefully designed, capable of producing life.* Now, *Jeremiah 33:25* states: '*But I, the Lord, have a covenant with day and night, and I have made the laws that control earth and sky.'*

Furthermore, *the atheist Francis Crick* stated the following in *'Life Itself: Its Origin and Nature, 1981.'* p. 88: *'An honest man, armed with all the knowledge available to us now, could only state that in some sense, the origin of life appears at the moment to be almost a 'miracle,' so much are the conditions which would have had to be satisfied to get it going.'*

A byline from the excellent article, posted on *October 29, 2021* by *Mario Seiglie* titled *'Seven Scientific Proofs of God'* follows : *'In the last 60 years, biologists have found that life began with an enormous amount of precise information already embedded in the cell. The human genome alone is a molecule with approximately three billion genetic letters, all precisely ordered to give instructions to the cell... From the most primitive cells to human beings, all have the same basic operating system of mind-boggling complexity with codes, transmitters and receivers, all working together.'*

At the end of this chapter, please find, as per the appreciated authorization by the United Church of God, the full article of *2021,* by *Mario Seiglie* titled *'Seven Scientific Proofs of God':*

Biochemist Michael Denton describes the cell this way: *'To grasp the reality of life, as it had been revealed by molecular biology, we must magnify a cell a billion times until it is twenty kilometres in diameter and resembles a giant airship, large enough to cover a great city like London or New York. What we would then see would be an object of unparalleled complexity and adaptive design... with all sorts of robot-like machines... the simplest of the functional components of the cell, the protein molecules are: astonishingly complex pieces of molecular machinery, each one consisting of about three thousand atoms, arranged in a highly organized 3-D conformation.*

This is why biochemists have a hard time believing and explaining that blind evolution could have constructed such machinery – and get all the parts to function together from the start. Additionally, to keep the human body functioning, biologists calculate that about 330 billion cells are replaced daily, equivalent to about 1 percent of all our cells (Mark Fischetti, 'Our bodies Replace Billions of Cells Every Day'; Scientific American, April 1, 2021).

Well, if you still question God's Existence, despite all the data submitted above, you could be in good company, despite:

- *The Wall Street Journal reference of December 25, 2014, as follows: 'Science Increasingly Makes the Case for GOD!'*

- *Einstein's comment: 'The most incomprehensible thing about the universe is that it is comprehensible!'*

- *Douglas Eli's recent book of 2020, titled: 'Proofs of God, A Conversation Between Reason and Doubt.' Douglas Eli is an MIT graduate in mathematics and physics, with a degree in Law. He was a long time non-believer who traces his 30-year journey – following the evidence of science – from atheism to belief – in yet a previous book in 2014, titled 'Counting on God, A Personal Journey Through Science to Belief.' Eli apparently used scrupulous analysis and probability calculations to make a convincing case that the most advanced, sophisticated thinking in science, not only allows for the idea of a designed universe, but encourages it. He adds the* *adage that says, <u>numbers don't lie</u>. In his book, 'Counting on God,' Eli applies <u>tens of mathematical analyses to recent scientific discoveries</u>, drawing startling conclusions.*

- *<u>Sir James Jeans</u>, one of the great astronomers of the 20th century who remarked in '<u>The Mysterious Universe</u>,' 1930, pp. 134, 137, that 'From the intrinsic evidence of his creation, <u>the Great Architect of the Universe</u> begins to appear as a <u>pure mathematician</u>... The universe begins to look more like a <u>great thought</u> than like a great machine. Incredibly, the universe has been found to be <u>mathematically designed</u>. It follows <u>orderly laws</u> that can be described in <u>mathematical terms</u>.'*

- *<u>Ross Douthat's</u> article in the <u>New York Times</u> of <u>August 14, 2021</u>, titled '<u>Finding Faith</u>.'*

- *<u>Albert Einstein's</u> statement that '<u>Coincidence is God's way of remaining anonymous</u>.'*

<u>Finally, as promised, is the</u> *2021 full article* by <u>Mario Seiglie</u> titled '<u>Seven Scientific Proofs of God</u>' (www.ucg.org):

In an increasingly secular society, many people today, especially those in public school or higher education, face intense pressure to reject belief in God. In most colleges and universities, especially in the Western world, a great many young men and women who start out believing in God will eventually end up denying His existence. They are not prepared for the barrage of arguments from textbooks and classes taught by atheist and agnostic teachers.

What can be done to avoid such tragic results? One key element is to educate and equip yourself and young people with arguments and answers to counter the attacks against belief in God they will encounter.

What does the evidence show?

Ironically, as scientific discovery has progressed, the evidence for God's existence has actually grown stronger rather than weaker, although most of the media and educational institutions will not readily admit it. One exception was a recent article in The New York Times' opinion page, where Ross Dou that made the case that there are "important ways in which the progress of science and the experience of modernity have strengthened the reasons to entertain the idea of God" ("A Guide to Finding Faith," Aug. 14, 2021, emphasis added throughout).

He explains: "The great project of modern physics, for instance, has led to speculation about a multiverse in part because it has repeatedly confirmed the strange fittedness of our universe to human life. If science has discredited certain specific ideas about how God structured the natural world, it has also made the mathematical beauty of physical laws, as well as their seeming calibration for the emergence of life, much clearer to us than they were to people 500 years ago."

Intelligent Design pioneer Dr. Stephen Meyer, discussed elsewhere in this issue, adds: "The major developments in science in the past five decades have been running in a strongly theistic direction. Science, done right, points toward God" (quoted by Lee Strobel, The Case for a Creator, 2004, p. 77).

It's vital to have faith in God's existence (Hebrews 11:6). Yet this is not a blind faith, but one that's based on clear evidence in creation all around us (Romans 1:20).

Scientists might be reluctant to admit it, but they are finding it harder to deny the overall picture of a carefully designed and purposeful universe.

Douglas Ell, an MIT graduate in math and physics who also holds a law degree, was previously a longtime skeptic about God. Yet no longer. He explains in his 2014 book Counting to God: A Personal Journey Through Science to Belief why he now accepts the existence of God: "Modern science has revealed a universe of absolute wonder. Wonder in the sense of awe, astonishment, surprise, and admiration. Wonder in what caused our universe to come into being; wonder in why our universe is designed just right for life, wonder in how the incredible complexity of even the simplest life could possibly have arisen.

"Each year brings new scientific evidence of wonder, facts for which there are essentially no explanations without God, no believable way around the wonder. Contrary to what you may have read, and contrary to what you may believe, science and religion are converging on wonder. The universe is a marvel to behold, and both scientists and religious believers are in awe of its magnificent design" (pp. 13-14).

Ell published a newer book in 2020 titled Proofs of God: A Conversation Between Reason and Doubt. Though written for teens and young adults, its clear and compelling case for a Creator is highly recommended to all.

The evidence for intelligent creation continues to mount. Here we'll look at seven scientific findings that prove the existence of God.

1. Science has discovered ample evidence that the universe had a beginning.

The scientific consensus 100 years ago was that the universe was eternal. This idea began to unravel with the implications of Albert Einstein's Theory of Relativity back in 1916, where his equations pointed to an expanding universe. Yet he didn't like that outcome and so added a constant to his equation that nullified the expansion. Later, he admitted it had been the biggest mathematical blunder in his life.

Then in 1929 astronomer Edwin Hubble affirmed he saw galaxies expanding outward, which meant they had been much closer together in the past. Einstein, intrigued, wanted to see the evidence for himself and in 1931 he visited the Mt. Wilson Observatory in Los Angeles, Calif. Einstein peered through the telescope, examined the evidence and then concluded, "I now see the necessity of a beginning." This started a change in the scientific attitude toward the cosmos.

Decades after, in 1965, two U.S. scientists detected the remnants of the initial burst of energy of the creation event typically called the "Big Bang." They both won a Nobel Prize in physics. One of them, Arno Penzias, later declared, "The best data we have [about the Big Bang] are exactly what I would have predicted had I nothing to go on but the first five books of Moses, the Psalms and the Bible as a whole" ("Clues to Universe Origin Expected," The New York Times, March 12, 1978, p. 1).

With the evidence at hand, what was written in Genesis 1:1 truly shocked many scientists by its accuracy: "In the beginning, God created the heavens and the earth." Here it says the universe of matter and energy appeared at a certain point in time and was all created by a Supreme Creator who existed before all of this happened. It was a huge proof of God's existence, with no real alternative explanations for a universe that, according to modern physics, appeared out of nothing.

2. Science has found the universe to be fine-tuned for life.

Almost 50 years ago, in 1973, cosmologist Brandon Carter found that the independent constants or laws in physics have one highly unusual characteristic in common—they are precisely the values needed to establish and sustain a universe capable of producing life. This is another enormous and virtually uncontested proof for a universe that has been carefully designed.

Scientists have found some 30 constants or laws of physics that govern the universe. All are unrelated to each other and yet are finely tuned to incredible proportions to make life possible. The evidence points to "Someone" spending a lot of time tuning all of these laws so they would work in unison.

Remarkably, the Bible revealed this truth long before any scientist discovered these facts. As Jeremiah 33:25 states, "But I, the Lord, have a covenant with day and night, and I have made the laws that control earth and sky" (Good News Translation).

3. Scientists can't explain the origin of life and its genetic code apart from an Originator.

Contrary to what many have been led to believe, scientists have no realistic explanation for how life arose.

Even the famous atheist and evolutionist Richard Dawkins admitted regarding the appearance of life, "Nobody knows how it happened" (Climbing Mount Improbable, 1996, p. 282). Furthermore, one of the discoverers of the DNA code, the atheist Francis Crick, concluded, "An honest man, armed with all the knowledge available to us now, could only state that in some sense, the origin of life appears at the moment to be almost a miracle, so many are the conditions which would have had to have been satisfied to get it going" (Life Itself: Its Origin and Nature, 1981, p. 88).

In the last 60 years, biologists have found that life began with an enormous amount of precise information already embedded in the cell. The human genome alone is a molecule with approximately 3 billion genetic letters, all precisely ordered to give instructions to the cell. Moreover, scientists have never found inorganic matter to create a coded system of information and the machinery to interpret it. From the most primitive cells to human beings, all have the same basic operating system of mind-boggling complexity, with codes, transmitters and receivers all working together.

In addition, the origin of life puzzle has a "chicken-and-egg question"—which came first, the chicken or the egg? In this case, to get life to occur, you need both the complete genetic code and the proteins—the machine parts—that read the code and build new proteins. Without the code, you can't build proteins. And without proteins, you can't process the code. So how could both have arisen at the same time?

4. Science has proven that biological life runs by millions of exquisitely programmed "robotic machines."

To understand what is happening inside a cell, a good illustration is picturing a large city teeming with life and movement.

Biochemist Michael Denton describes the cell this way: "To grasp the reality of life as it has been revealed by molecular biology, we must magnify a cell a billion times until it is twenty kilometers in diameter and resembles a giant airship large enough to cover a great city like London or New York. What we would then see would be an object of unparalleled complexity and adaptive design . . .

"We would see around us, in every direction we looked, all sorts of robot-like machines. We would notice that the simplest of the functional components of the cell, the protein molecules, were astonishingly complex pieces of molecular machinery, each one consisting of about three thousand atoms arranged in highly organized 3-D spatial conformation.

"We would wonder even more as we watched the strangely purposeful activities of these weird molecular machines, particularly when we realized that, despite all our accumulated knowledge of physics and chemistry, the task of designing one such molecular machine—that is one single functional protein molecule—would be completely beyond our capacity at present" (Evolution: A Theory in Crisis, 1986, p. 329).

This is why biochemists have a hard time believing and explaining that blind evolution can construct such machinery—and get all the parts to function together from the start. Additionally, to keep the human body functioning, biologists calculate that "about 330 billion cells are replaced daily, equivalent to about 1 percent of all our cells" (Mark Fischetti, "Our Bodies Replace Billions of Cells Every Day," Scientific American, April 1, 2021).

"We take life for granted," adds Douglas Ell, "because it is everywhere. Our planet is overrun by biological machines. There are at least 10 million different types (species) of machines; some estimate that tens of millions of other types (species) have not yet been discovered...

"Coordinated systems allow blue whales to dive thousands of feet below sea level without being crushed and sing complex songs that travel across oceans. Other systems allow bees to do a dance that tells other bees where to find the best sources of pollen. There are systems for hiding, systems for fighting, systems for reproducing, systems for getting food, systems for communicating, and so on" (Counting to God, p. 110).

Such discoveries show that everything about life is programmed to the last detail and that virtually nothing has been left to chance. Does this exquisite design point to evolution or to God? The answer is obvious.

5. Science has found the earliest evidence of life to be of great variety, fully formed and without transitions.

Though Darwin titled his book On the Origin of Species by Means of Natural Selection, he was never able to substantiate that assumption. Many people assume that the theory of evolution, with its countless mutations and natural selection as the means of *change, can account for the origin and development of all the living things on this planet.*

Yet this is sleight of hand, since evolution can account for microevolution, or changes within the species (such as dogs of varying sizes, shapes and colors), but not macroevolution, or changes from one kind of creature to another. Natural selection can tell you something about the survival of the species, but nothing about the arrival of the species. It certainly cannot trace the origin of the approximately 10 million species on earth. These are classified into some 33 main body types or phyla, such as sponges, worms, insects and mammals.

Darwin predicted that as more of the fossil record was uncovered, it would show types of species gradually appearing, beginning with one or a few, and then multiplying from simple to more complex life forms. He wrote, "If numerous species... have really started into life at once, the fact would be fatal to the theory of evolution through natural selection" (Origin of Species, 1859, p. 305). Yet that is precisely what has been found—major body types appearing at what's considered the beginning of the fossil record rather than in deposits laid down later.

Scientists call this "the Cambrian Explosion," referring to major types of plants and animals suddenly appearing fully formed in that fossil layer. This is the opposite of what Darwin and evolutionists had claimed would be found—and they have no real explanation or answers. Of the 33 main body types, 23 of them (or 70%) appear at the recognized beginning stage of the fossil record.

What we are talking about here, by analogy, would be like find-
ing together such different inventions as a washing machine, a
refrigerator, a bicycle, a car and an airplane. Although they do
have some features in common, they have very distinct functions
and purposes. Similarly, the major types of creatures found in the
Cambrian layer, such as sponges, worms, trilobites and jawless fish,
are quite diverse, complex and appear suddenly, with no evidence
of these main body types evolving from other creatures.

As paleontologist Niles Eldredge admitted: "If life had evolved
into the wondrous profusion of creatures little by little, then there
should be some fossiliferous record of those changes... But no one
has found any evidence of such in-between creatures... All of the
fossil evidence to date has failed to turn up any such missing
links" (George Alexander, "Alternate Theory of Evolution Consid-
ered," Los Angeles Times, Nov. 19, 1978).

Yes, Darwin has been let down by the fossil record!

6. Science has shown the earth to be a unique planet with so many
"just right" conditions to sustain life.

In 1966, Carl Sagan hosted the famous TV documentary series Cos-
mos. He thought in order to have life you just needed two condi-
tions—a right kind of star and a planet at the right distance. This
conclusion proved to be totally off base.

Now, more than half a century later, scientists have come to the re-
alization that more than 200 conditions have to be "just right" for
life to exist and thrive. As author Eric Metaxas explains: "Today
there are more than 200 known parameters necessary for a planet

to support life—every single one of which must be perfectly met, or the whole thing falls apart. Without a massive planet like Jupiter nearby, whose gravity will draw away asteroids, a thousand times as many would hit Earth's surface. The odds against life in the universe are simply astonishing" ("Science Increasingly Makes the Case for God," The Wall Street Journal, Dec. 25, 2014).

The Bible tells us: "The Lord is God. He made the skies and the earth. He put the earth in its place. He did not want the earth to be empty when he made it. He created it to be lived on. I am the Lord. There is no other God" (Isaiah 45:18, Easy-to-Read Version).

7. Science reveals the universe is precisely mathematically designed while allowing for free will.

Incredibly, the universe has been found to be mathematically designed. It follows orderly laws that can be described in mathematical terms. Sir James Jeans, one of the great astronomers of the 20th century, remarked: "From the intrinsic evidence of his creation, the Great Architect of the Universe now begins to appear as a pure mathematician... The universe begins to look more like a great thought than like a great machine" (The Mysterious Universe, 1930, pp. 134, 137).

A big problem for evolutionists and atheists is this: Evolution can't do math, since it is based on random variations and mutations, and math requires an intelligent agent who can first prepare a mathematical blueprint of laws before creating things so they will be orderly. This is why the present cosmos can be traced back to mathematical rules.

As Einstein noted, "The most incomprehensible thing about the universe is that it is comprehensible." He meant that it could be understood in mathematical terms but that an explanation for that was beyond math.

As far back as the early 1900s, scientists were discovering the laws that govern the subatomic realm, the tiny microcosm described by quantum mechanics. It has very different rules than our macro world and appears to make room for such things as free will to arise.

Many scientists came to realize that not all is determined by matter and energy. Experiments show that an observer can alter a particle through means of observing it. The implications are that we can determine the outcome of our lives by the choices we make.

It brings to mind what God said: "Today I have given you a choice between life and death, success and disaster. I command you today to love the Lord your God. I command you to follow him and to obey his commands, laws, and rules. Then you will live..." (Deuteronomy 30:15-16, ERV).

What do we learn from this?

Science offers many proofs from our physical universe that point to the existence of God. We've looked here at seven. And cutting-edge science is constantly revealing more complexity and deeper design, not only in the cosmos, but also in all living things.

The biblical patriarch Job once challenged skeptics to look at the design of the creatures around them and notice they witness to a Supreme Designer and Creator. He stated: "Even birds and animals have much they could teach you; ask the creatures of earth and sea *for their wisdom. All of them know that the Lord's hand made them" (Job 12:7-9, GNT).*

Consequently, by examining all the evidence and realizing where it leads, we hope you will believe in God, will keep believing, and will earnestly seek His will for your life!'

I REST MY CASE!

5

GOD'S MERCY / JUSTICE.

Allow me to start with the obvious: _God's mercy goes way beyond any human comprehension_. Numerous examples of this _incommensurable divine mercy_ are repeatedly referenced in a number of parables, including: _The Prodigal Son_ (Lk 15:11-32), _The Workers in the Vineyard_ (Mt 20:1-16) and the _Lost Sheep_ (Lk 15:4), among numerous other manifestations of this _utterly disproportionate mercy._

Well, we mortals, while being _somewhat aware_ of this divine grace, tend to _question its validity_ by opposing it to God's _justice_, penalizing the wrongdoers; this too is referenced in the Bible and in other religions. Such references tend to second our _mortal mentality_ of _human judgement_ and _revenge_. Accordingly, this also tends to _validate the outcome of hell and purgatory_ which will be dealt with in a subsequent chapter. In the meantime, allow me to quote a reference by _Pernot_ to _Hitler_ which concludes this chapter, as follows:

'We will not meet Hitler in Heaven because Hitler will no longer be Hitler, then; he will have rid himself of his folly and of his monstrosity.'

This quote is seconded by a corresponding one from _Saint John of the Cross_, as mentioned in a previous chapter, as follows:

'God sustains every soul and dwells in it substantially, even though it be that of the greatest sinner in the world, and this union is natural.'

Why would we agree that _Hitler in Heaven would no longer be Hitler_, and that _God dwells substantially in every soul, though it be that of the greatest sinner in the world_, without admitting to _God's incommensurable mercy_?

I, for one, admit that the evidence is outstanding, but allow me to add my grain of salt, as follows:

Numerous scientific studies indicate that one's _human 'conscience' survives the biological death of our bodies for a certain while_; one of them is as follows:

'Consciousness after clinical death. The biggest ever scientific study published:

Southampton University scientists have found evidence that 'awareness' continues for at least several minutes after clinical death which was previously thought impossible.

A recent article in the British newspaper The Daily Mail featured an interview with Dr. Sam Parnia, with the lead:

"Consciousness may continue even after death. Sam Parnia is head of a multidisciplinary team at Southampton University (United Kingdom) who published a study in the Official Journal of Euro-

pean Resuscitation Council, with the title "AWARE—AWAreness during REsuscitation—A prospective

(DOI: http://dx.doi.org/10.1016/j.resuscitation.2014.09.004)

which included more than 2,000 persons who suffered a cardiac arrest and successfully responded to a resuscitation treatment, in 15 hospitals in the United Kingdom, United States and Austria. This is the largest study of its kind to date, using a rigorous methodology, in order to exclude all those cases that could be based on individual impressions that are worthy, but which hold no scientific interest.

Jerry Nolan, Editor-in-Chief at Resuscitation Journal, who did not participate in the study but is considered an authority on the subject, said of the research, "Dr. Parnia and his colleagues are to be congratulated on the completion of a fascinating study that will open the door to more extensive research into what happens when we die.

CONSCIOUSNESS AFTER CLINICAL DEATH : WHETHER IT FADES AWAY AFTERWARDS, WE DO NOT KNOW.

The results revealed that 40% of those who survived a cardiac arrest were aware during the time that they were clinically dead and before their hearts were restarted. Dr. Parnia, in the interview stated: The evidence thus far suggests that in the first few minutes after death, consciousness is not annihilated.

Now with such as a confirmed fact, allow me to add my personal reflection on the input of our *All-Merciful God* Who undoubtedly *would seize the opportunity of our continued limited conscience to intervene* in our favour, 'though it be that of the greatest sinner in *the world.'* Just as was clear in the three aforementioned parables, God would *certainly refuse the plea of the oldest son* in that of the *'Prodigal Son,'* as well as that of the earliest *'workers in the vineyard,'* and would *go after every 'lost sheep' left behind,* offering a *last minute pledge of salvation*: to finally say *yes to a promise of paradise* that *Christ died for*. My reflection is one of a *mortal father and grandpa*; even more so of our *Heavenly Father* Whose *justice is one of incalculable love* and *forgiveness, beyond every aspect of our human fragility and unworthiness!*

My reflection on God's mercy, as opposed to His justice, seems to be in line with a number of articles on the Web, including one in the *La Croix* magazine, titled:

'When justice means mercy - La Croix

https://international.lacroix.com/news/religion/when-justice-means-mercy/9832 Web 2019-04-06.

One other recent article sums it all up, as follows:

'How Does God's Mercy and Justice Work Together in Salvation?'

https://www.christianity.com/wiki/salvation/how-does-gods-mercy-and-justice-work-together-in-salvation.html Web 2021-05-03.

And so, *in mercy, God sent his Son to receive in himself the judgment demanded by God's righteousness. God's mercy and justice came together on Calvary* when *Jesus, God incarnate, bore in his flesh the punishment we all deserved.* And *he did that so that all who would believe in him might have eternal life.'*

Conclusion:

God does not in any way act as a judge or an accountant. God's justice is that of a father or grandpa, deeply in love of His children and grandkids; He follows His Divine Heart with a _JUSTICE OF LOVE!_

Question yourselves as parents or grandparents: _how would you act towards your kids or grandkids who go astray? Aristotle_ responds on your behalf, as follows: _'Asking the right question is half the answer.'_

This _'half answer'_ is for _'humans'; how much more categorical_ would the _'full answer' be from God, the All-Merciful?_ Do you still harbor any doubts? I certainly do not!

6

HEAVEN, HELL & PURGATORY.

Based on the facts mentioned in the previous chapter, allow me to conclude that _hell does not exist_, and that _most of us, if not all, will go straightforward to Heaven_, because _Christ's death on the Cross saved us – ALL of us, regardless of our beliefs_, be they Christian or not! This fact also applies to _atheists_ and _agnostics!_

I am also basing my conviction on an excerpt from the Parable of the hundred sheep (Luke 15:4-5) and on John 6:37-38, as follows:

'What man among you, if he has a hundred sheep and loses one of them, does not leave the ninety-nine in the pasture and go after the one that is lost, until he finds it? And when he finds it, he joyfully puts it on his shoulders.'

Accordingly, _ALL 100 SHEEP; NONE EXCLUDED!_

The answer is _'NO' for humans_, but _'YES' for God_!

'_All those the Father gives me will come to me_, and _whoever comes to me I will never drive away_. For I have come down from heaven not to do my will but to do the will of him who sent me.'

Well, you may rightfully ask me about _Purgatory_; _I admit my hesitancy to accept such a passage_, prior to Heaven, unless _Purgatory replaces Hell_, namely _yet another chance_ of _Salvation_, offered by our _All-Merciful Divine Father_ to all those who, during the period of _consciousness, following the death of their bodies, continue to say 'NO' to Paradise!_ Truly _inconceivable but possible_ with stubborn beings; even those brothers and sisters would in no way be sent _for ever_ to a _burning furnace of hell_, but would be held in _Purgatory, a neutral transition, to allow them to change their obstinate minds_!

In fact, the _Orthodox Church_ refuses the notion of Purgatory, for the simple reason that there is _no mention of it in the Bible_; in fact, the Bible suggests _the opposite_; Jesus Himself said so in _Luke 22:39-43_, as follows:

'One of the _criminals_ who hung there hurled insults at him: "Aren't you the Messiah? Save yourself and us!"'

But the other criminal rebuked him. "Don't you fear God," he said, "since you are under the same sentence? We are punished justly, for we are getting what our deeds deserve. But this man has done nothing wrong."

Then he said, _"Jesus, remember me when you come into your kingdom."_

Jesus answered him, "Truly I tell you, _today you will be with me in paradise."_

Jesus thereby confirms to the good _criminal laron's call_, indicating the _immediacy_ of his entering the _Kingdom of God: 'TODAY,'_ not following an eventual purification act in Purgatory.

Accordingly, please always keep in mind that _God's Mercy surpasses by far our human comprehension_; Jesus reconfirms this fact in yet another text in John's Gospel (1 John 3:20), as follows:

'If our hearts condemn us, we know that God is greater than our hearts, and he knows everything.'

Thereby, _grace is more powerful than sin_ and _Divine Love is far greater than judgment!_

Before discussing God's Kingdom in Heaven, let's first delve into what Jesus responded to _Nicodemus_, as per John _3: 1-3_, as follows:

'Jesus replied, "Very truly I tell you, _no one can see the kingdom of God unless they are born again._"'

Now, what does Jesus' response tell us about our _new birth after the death of our bodies_, as per:

Ecclesiastes 12:7,

'...before the dust returns to the ground from which it came and the spirit returns to God who gave it.'

Now, once _our spirit (soul) returns to its Source (the Holy Spirit, God),_ and _our bodies (dust) return to the ground from which it came_, a question arises as to _which part of us would wait for redemption in Purgatory or burn in the furnace of hell_? To me, the answer is obvious: _neither our soul nor our body_! Have I managed to convince you or should I expect a different response from the Church or from any of you, readers, who are part of the Church or of any other religious body? Atheists or Agnostics? Any one?

Back to the *Kingdom of God, Heaven, Paradise, the New Eden.* **Is this a *precise location*, *beyond the clouds*, up there where God, Saints and Angels reside and which is unattainable for the living? *NO!***

An excerpt from the *introduction of this book* states the following: '*...do not point to a 'specific location up there,' 'unattainable to living humans,'* but to '*the whole*' of a '*refreshed universe*' *among the living and the dead of 'all generations, past, present and future,'* the dead having been transformed into '*saintly angels*,' surrounding the living, helping them to become in turn eventual '*angel-saints*,' upon their '*new birth*' *at the moment of their 'death.'*

Accordingly, *Heaven is a 'refreshed universe'* which *includes earth and the living* whereby our *transfigured selves* roam freely with no barriers, *as did Christ following His resurrection*, appearing to the *women who fetched his tomb*, to His *Apostles* and to the *Emmaus Disciples*, among others. *When we die, our mortal bodies disappear, being replaced by our 'transfigured entities'; what a relief for our loved ones* who *mourn our mortal loss*!

The Bible references our jubilation in *that refreshed universe*, as follows:

'The wolf will live with the lamb, the leopard will lie down with the goat, the calf and the lion and the yearling together; and a little child will lead them. The cow will feed with the bear, their young will lie down together, and the lion will eat straw like the ox. The infant will play near the cobra's den, and the young child will put its hand into the viper's nest. They will neither harm nor destroy on all my holy mountain, for the earth will be filled with the knowledge of the Lord as the waters cover the sea.' (Isaiah 11:6-9)

'On this mountain the Lord Almighty will prepare a feast of rich food for all peoples, a banquet of aged wine—the best of meats and the finest of wines. On this mountain he will destroy the shroud that enfolds all peoples, the sheet that covers all nations; he will swallow up death forever. The Sovereign <u>Lord</u> will wipe away the tears from all faces; he will remove his people's disgrace from all the earth. The Lord has spoken.' (Isaiah 25 :6-8)

'Your dead will live; their bodies will rise. Awake and sing, you who dwell in the dust! For your dew is like the dew of the morning, and the earth will bring forth her dead.' (Isaiah 26-19)

'He will wipe away every tear from their eyes, and death shall be no more, neither shall there be mourning, nor crying, nor pain anymore, for the former things have passed away.' (Revelations 21:4).

<u>CONCLUSIONS :</u>

Heaven, Paradise, the Celestial Kingdom are <u>*all over the universe, including the earth and the sky above it*</u>; in fact in the Lord's Prayer, Jesus called on us to pray that:

<u>*'Thy kingdom come. Thy will be done on earth as it is in heaven.'*</u>

Was His reference to <u>*His Kingdom*</u> *'on earth as it is in heaven'* a coincidence? I do not think so because <u>*God is everywhere*</u>, <u>*as are the souls of the living and the dead*</u>: *celestial sparks* in the former and <u>*integral parts of the Holy Spirit, God*</u>, in the latter, *once liberated from their mortal bodies at the very instant of death.*

It is thereby also obvious that _we continue to exist after the death of our bodies_; we are _by the side of our loved ones, just as Jesus was with His beloved, following His resurrection_, as per _John 20:19_:

'Then the same day at evening, being the first day of the week, when the doors were shut where the disciples were assembled for fear of the Jews, came Jesus and stood in the midst, and saith unto them, Peace be unto you.'

Accordingly, _no barriers will block our way: no doors, no walls, no distance, no time! We will always be available, in support of our beloved, on earth._ We could also _be in more than one place at a time_, just like many Saints were in bi-locations during their lifetimes; one example is that of _Padre Pio (1887-1968)_.

Our souls will be enveloped by transfigured bodies, just like Jesus was, according to _Luke 9, 28-36_:

'Now about eight days after these sayings he took with him _Peter and John and James_ and went up on the mountain to pray. And as he was praying, _the appearance of his face was altered, and his clothing became dazzling white_. And behold, two men were talking with him, _Moses and Elijah_, who _appeared in glory_ and _spoke of his departure, which he was about to accomplish at Jerusalem_. Now Peter and those who were with him were heavy with sleep, but when they became fully awake _they saw his glory_ and the two men who stood with him. And as the men were parting from him, Peter said to Jesus, "Master, it is good that we are here. Let us make _three tents, one for you and one for Moses and one for Elijah_" — not knowing what he said. As he was saying these things, _a cloud came and overshadowed them_, and they were afraid as they entered the cloud. And a voice came out of the cloud, saying, "*This is my Son, my Chosen One; listen to him!*" And when the voice had spoken, Jesus was found alone. And they kept silent and told no one in those days anything of what they had seen.'

Correspondingly, <u>*our souls*</u>, once liberated from our mortal bodies, will be <u>*transfigured*</u> into <u>*mystic entities*</u>, <u>*in the very same way that Jesus*</u>, *Moses and Elijah* were portrayed in Luke's above text; we will constitute the *Communion of Saints*, referenced in the latter part of the *Creed*:

'I believe in the <u>*Holy Spirit*</u>;

the <u>*Holy Catholic Church*</u>;

the <u>*Communion of Saints*</u>;

the <u>*forgiveness of sins*</u>;

the <u>*resurrection of the body*</u>;

and the <u>*life everlasting*</u>. Amen.'

The Apostles' Creed refers to the <u>*communion of the saints in reference to all believers, past and present*</u>, <u>*who share in the salvation, thanks to Jesus Christ*</u>. This includes <u>*deceased Christians*</u> who <u>*live with Christ today*</u> <u>*and those still alive*</u>. This affirms <u>*one salvation*</u> (*Ephesians 2:8-9; Acts 4:12*) that <u>*applies to all people*</u> (*Christians and non Christians, believers and atheists and agnostics – ALL*).

The above underlined texts of the Creed confirm the beliefs, described in this book, including the fact that <u>*we will continue an*</u>

active life after our death, as promised by *Saint Thérèse of Lisieux*, as follows:

"...I will spend my Heaven doing good on earth."

The identity of our soul after the death of the body and the existence of God (Holy Spirit or Supersoul) is also described in other faiths, as with Bhagavad-Gita (5th century B.C.):

"I am seated in everyone's heart as the all pervading Supersoul and from Me comes remembrance, knowledge, and forgetfulness."
~ Bhagavad Gita 15:15

"For the soul there is neither birth nor death at any time. He has not come into being, does not come into being, and will not come into being. He is unborn, eternal, ever-existing and primeval. He is not slain when the body is slain." ~ Bhagavad Gita 2.20

"Only the material body is perishable; the embodied soul within is indestructible, immeasurable, and eternal." ~ Bhagavad Gita 2.18.

"As a person sheds worn-out garments and wears new ones, likewise, at the time of death, the soul casts off its worn-out body and enters a new one." ~ Bhagavad Gita 2.22.

"Death is certain for one who has been born, and rebirth is inevitable for one who has died." ~ Bhagavad Gita 2.27.

Wisdom at its best, five centuries B.C.; a reflection of this great wisdom was echoed by Greek and Roman thinkers like *Socrates, Plato, Virgile and Plotinus.*

7

DOGMAS / MYSTERIES / PAPAL INFALLIBILITY.

With all due respect to _my Church_, I am fully cognisant of my risking _excommunication_ for my _deviations from the Catechetic principles_ by duly declaring some doubt as to the principle of _imposing unalterable dogmas_, _unexplained mysteries_ and _taking for granted the papal infallibility_.

I am a believer in the _benefits of 'doubt'_ which are essential in all spheres of life, _including faith. Doubt is the motor of moving forward, of thought, of discovery, of knowledge, of progress, of creation, of comprehension, of wisdom, of truth, of hope, of our very spirit! We need to be aware of our ignorance_ and of _the need to feed and nourish our deficiencies through doubt_, in order _to attain wisdom and truth_; this truth could be subjected to _further doubt in order to clarify it further_. It is through doubt that we could get the ball rolling, thereby _avoiding our intellectual paralysis, both moral and religious_.

Two quotations from _Friedrich Nietzche_ shed light on my stand, as follows:

'Not doubt, but certainty is what drives us insane.'

'Christianity has done its utmost to close the circle and <u>declared</u> <u>even doubt to be sin</u>. One is supposed to be <u>cast into belief without</u> <u>reason</u>, by a miracle, and from then on to swim in it as in the brightest and least ambiguous of elements... What is wanted are blindness and intoxication and an eternal song over <u>the waves in</u> <u>which reason has drowned.'</u>

I am also an adept of <u>*René Descartes*</u>, with respect to the principle of '<u>*Cartesian doubt*</u>'; he <u>*put all beliefs, ideas, thoughts, and matter*</u> <u>*in doubt*</u>'; he demonstrated that '<u>*his grounds, or reasoning,*</u> *for any knowledge <u>could just as well be false</u>. <u>Sensory experience, the</u>* <u>*primary mode of knowledge, is often erroneous and therefore must*</u> <u>*be doubted*</u>' as follows:

'<u>*I think, Therefore I am.*</u>' *(Cogito, ergo sum.)*

'<u>*I will devote myself sincerely and without reservation to the general*</u> <u>*demolition of my opinions*</u>. *What better way to spend the night?'*

But <u>Descartes</u> was not without reason: in his work as a <u>mathe-</u> <u>*matician*</u>, *he worried that <u>if the foundations of knowledge were</u>* <u>*not completely solid, anything built upon them would inevitably*</u> <u>*collapse*</u>. *He thus decided that <u>if there was reason to doubt the truth</u>* <u>*of something — no matter how slim the doubt — then it should be*</u> <u>*discarded as false.'*</u>

To that wisdom of Descartes' he is seconded by <u>*Confucius*</u>, as follows:

<u>*He who knows not, and knows not he knows not, is a fool; shun him.*</u>

He who knows not, and knows he knows not, is a student; teach him.

He who knows, and knows not he knows, is asleep; awaken him.

He who knows, and knows he knows, is wise; follow him.'

"He who knows all the answers has not been asked all the questions."

Back to my thinking; I do not believe I am a *fool* or *asleep*, and I am certainly not that *wise*; I am but a *student seeking* answers by declaring my *doubts* and *sharing them* with others that could be *asleep*, attempting to awaken them to have them accompany me in my reflections.

One thing is certain: we need to *listen to and trust the Holy Spirit Who is in every one of our souls and Who continues to teach us and accompany us* all through our lifetimes, as per *John 14, 16-17*:

'And I will ask the Father, and he will give you *another advocate* to *help you and be with you forever* — the *Spirit of truth*. The world cannot accept him, because it neither sees him nor knows him. But *you know him*, for *he lives with you and will be in you*.'

Accordingly, *stagnation — including spiritual —* is a roadblock, an asphyxia, a bottleneck, a paralysis, leading to a *blockage of fluidity, of growth, of progress, of further understanding our faith*; Jesus Himself confirmed that *evolution of our comprehension of His teachings*, as per *John 16, 12-13*:

'*I have MUCH MORE to say to you, more than you can now bear.*But when he, the *Spirit of truth*, comes, *he will guide you into ALL the truth*. He will not speak on his own; he will speak only what he hears, and he will tell you *what is YET TO COME*.'

Accordingly, *the Gospel is NOT static; it EVOLVES constantly in time, under the NEW teachings (WHAT IS TO COME – John 16:13) by the Holy Spirit*. Besides, that *Holy Spirit is in each one of us; Popes do not hold a monopoly* of such *NEW TRUTHS!*

Meanwhile, the Catechism teaches us the *PERMANANCE OF DOGMAS*, in that *a dogma established by a Pope cannot be revised or annulled by another, no matter the evolution of teachings* and *any new truths, yet to come*, inspired by the Holy Spirit, *unknown to the previous Pope* who established the dogma!

Moreover, our Church *has not always had good Popes! I therefore disagree with the infallibility of Popes.*

As to spiritual *mysteries*, the *Merriam Webster dictionary definition, as follows: 'a religious truth that one can know only by revelation and cannot fully understand'* should not be necessarily applicable; there are either *explanations or doubts*. Previous chapters have detailed explanations of what a *soul* is, as well as *heaven, hell, purgatory, our partial divinity, our immortality* and many other taught mysteries! This is exactly what this book is about; *idem*, what *sermons* by the Pope, Cardinals, Bishops, Priests and deacons should attempt to do.

Accordingly, *mysteries are doubts to be clarified and certitudes to be established and understood by all*, as per *John 3:6*:

rebirth in the Spirit:

'Flesh gives birth to flesh,

but the Spirit gives birth to spirit.'

Remember, we are _ALL_ _reborn by the Spirit!_

8

THE OLD TESTAMENT

The Old Testament is the *Hebraic Bible* that precedes the arrival of Jesus Christ; in some respects, the *New Testament* represents the *fulfillment* of *some* of the *revelations* of the *Old Testament*. However, as a *word of caution*: *many of the stories of the latter are symbolic* in nature and *should in no way be taken as factual*. Unfortunately, they impact, not only our Sunday School Catechetic teachings of our children, but also some *dogmas* that are *rock solid and irreversible* in our Christian faith. A major example is in our belief that *Adam and Eve were indeed our foreparents* who lived in the *Garden of Eden* where they committed the *sin of disobedience to God* that *impacted and tainted every single newborn* ever since, along with *adults to date!* For example, *Pope Pius IX* proclaimed in *1854* the *dogma* of the *Immaculate Conception:* that *our Blessed Mother was free of the Original Sin* from the moment of her conception. Well, *no one contests that fact; I am, first and foremost, a believer in the Immaculate Conception*, not only of our Blessed Mother, but *also of every single other newborn*. I do so because of my firm refusal of a *hereditary sin*, committed by a *symbolic Adam and Eve*, ages ago!

This topic will be further discussed in a future chapter. However, in the meantime, allow me to deliver my belief to my readers with facts, dated *1950 and October 25, 1986*, as follows, as per *https:// www.spokesman.com:*

'In his most comprehensive statement yet on <u>evolution, *Pope John Paul II*</u> insisted that *<u>faith and science can coexist</u>*, telling scientists that *<u>Darwin's theories are sound</u>*, as long as they take into account that *<u>creation was the work of God</u>*.

The Pope's message to the *Pontifical Academy of Sciences, a lay organization* meeting in *Rome* this week, recalled how *<u>Pope Pius XII</u>* proclaimed in *<u>1950</u>* that the evolution doctrine was *a <u>serious hypothesis</u>*.

In the statement released Wednesday, the pope said new knowledge has *<u>confirmed that Charles Darwin's theory of evolution is more than a hypothesis</u>*. Darwin's theory — that humankind was the product of a *<u>slow evolutionary process from early forms of life</u>* — conflicts with the *<u>literal biblical account of creation,</u>* that the world, including humans, was *<u>created in six days</u>*.'

Accordingly, if <u>Adam & Eve</u> are <u>symbolic manifestations of Creation</u>, then our demonstrated <u>foreparents did not commit</u> that <u>Original Sin</u> that has stained every single newborn since, and which <u>spared our Blessed Virgin</u> who <u>evidently</u> was <u>born immaculate just like every other newborn</u>. The problem here is one that relates to *<u>DOGMAS THAT ARE IRREVOCABLE</u>*, despite the declared fact in *John 16:12 and John 14:26* that *<u>the Holy Spirit will keep teaching us new truths</u>*, as follows:

'I HAVE MUCH MORE TO SAY TO YOU, MORE THAN YOU CAN NOW BEAR'

'BUT THE HELPER, THE HOLY SPIRIT, WHOM THE FATHER WILL SEND IN MY NAME, HE WILL TEACH YOU ALL THINGS AND BRING TO YOUR REMEMBRANCE ALL THAT I HAVE SAID TO YOU'

The above represents the most outstanding evidence that *many* of the Old Testament stories are *symbolic in nature and are not to be believed literally.*

However, some are also *prophetic* in nature, illustrating *what is to come,* in the New Testament, *relative to Christ's presence among us;* one such example is that of the biblical account of *Jonas and the whale,* in *Jonah 1.* Could anyone believe the story that *'For three days, Jonah sat in the belly of the big fish. Then, God had the big fish throw up Jonah onto the shores of Nineveh?'* Even a child in Sunday School could draw a parallel between *Jonas' Old Testament story* and our Christian faith of *Christ's crucifixion and His resurrection on the third day.*

Moreover, one of the most primary prophecies that *is and always will be substantial in nature, is that* of the prophet *ISAIAH (Isaiah 7:14)* who declared that *JESUS WOULD BE BORN FROM A VIRGIN* AND THAT HIS NAME WOULD BE <u>IMMANUEL</u>: 'Therefore the <u>*LORD HIMSELF*</u> SHALL GIVE YOU *A SIGN*: BEHOLD, *A VIRGIN SHALL CONCEIVE,* AND *BEAR A SON,* AND SHALL CALL HIS NAME *IMMANUEL.'*

This prophecy which materialized with the birth of Jesus is a _cornerstone of our Christian faith, indeed fully and literally inspired by God_. It is accordingly fundamental for every one of us to identify and separate such _factual prophecies_ from many other stories in the Old Testament that call for _war, killings, genocide, extermination, beheading, stoning, rape of virgins and others, robbery and other mischievous acts_, all to be identified further in this chapter.

This other aspect of the Old Testament portrays God as an _instigator_ of _violence, killing and destruction_ of _enemies_, or at least _condones_ them; numerous examples of this _genocidal Yahweh_ are abhorrent, such as in the _flood_ (Genesis 6-8), _Sodom and Gomorrah_ (Genesis 18-19), calls for the _slaughter_ of all the Egyptian first-born sons (Exodus 12:29) and even commands Jews to _exterminate_ Canaanites (Deuteronomy 20:_17_, as well as numerous other references in the Old Testament). Numerous other _genocidal acts and massacres, apparently approved by Yahweh_, are part of the Old Testament _39 books_, such as: Joshua _exterminates_ the Anakim (Joshua 11:21-23), Elijah has _42 children killed_ (Kings 2:22-23), Elijah _burns to death_ 102 men (Kings 1:10-12), and last of numerous other references, the _killing of Hamor, his son, and all the men of their village, and taking their money, cattle, wives and children_ (Genesis 34:13-29). Moreover, the teachings of the Old Testament include death by _stoning_ (Numbers 15:32 & 15:36), _beheading_ (Numbers 25-4), and _mass rape of 32,000 virgins_, among numerous others (Numbers 31: 9 & 17-18).

Hate in the Old Testament is rampant, contrary to _love_ in the New Testament.

What is most disturbing to me, *a practicing Christian*, is the fact that <u>the first reading in the Holy Mass</u> is one from the *Old Testament*. I have to admit that I rarely — if ever — respond to the lector's invitation at the end of that reading, referring to it as '*The word of the Lord*,' by '*Thanks be to God*.' I refrain from doing so because I cannot and will not admit that *<u>our Loving Father inspired such hatred and utter violence.</u>*

<u>I take this opportunity to beg our Roman Catholic Church to follow the lead of the Oriental Churches, both Catholic and Orthodox, that dropped such readings from their Holy Masses.</u>

Back to the *symbolism*, portrayed in the Old Testament; one other example is the reference to *<u>Eve being born from Adam's rib</u>*. Well, we have already established that Adam and Eve did not exist, as such; so goes the story of the rib, in *Genesis 2 :21-24*:

'And the Lord God caused a deep sleep to fall upon Adam and he slept; and he took one of his ribs, and closed up the flesh instead thereof;

And the rib, which the Lord had taken from man, made him a woman, and brought her unto the man.

And Adam said, This is now bone of my bones, and flesh of my flesh; she shall be called Woman, because she was taken out of Man.

Therefore shall a man leave his father and his mother, and shall cleave unto his wife, and they shall be one flesh.'

Well, the fact is that men and women have the *<u>exact same number of ribs</u>*: an additional confirmation of the mere *symbolism* of the

64

story in the Old Testament which is simply prophesying the Gospel according to _John — Wedding in Cana:_

'On the third day there was a wedding in Cana in Galilee, and the mother of Jesus was there...'

The principles, portrayed above, are _applicable to the many other stories in the Old Testament_, such as _Noah's Ark, the Tower of Babel_, and so on and so forth.

I will end with a final note, referencing a _common concept_ in the _three Abrahamic religions — Judaism, Christianity and Islam_, namely the _symbol_ that _God created the world out of nothing — ex nihilo — contrary to the Darwinian concept of evolution._

9

IMMACULATE CONCEPTION, ASSUMPTION, TRANSFIGURATION.

Let me start by *declaring solemnly my utmost respect to the VIRGIN MARY, OUR HOLY MOTHER*, *recognised and glorified, not only by Christians, but also by Muslims* to whom they have devoted a complete chapter (*#19*) of the *Coran*, titled: *Surah Maryam, verse 35* among others, as follows (*SURAH MARYAM (MARY) – Quran in English*):

"O Maryam! Verily, Allah gives you the glad tidings of a 'Word' from Him, his name will be Al-Masih, 'Isa, the son of Maryam, held in honor in this world and in the Hereafter, and he will be one of those who are near to Allah."

... 'the messenger who brought our soul/divine message to her gave her an example of a perfect human being.'

The messenger/Zachariah said: "I am only the messenger of your Rabb to bestow you a pure boy."

Mary said: "How can I have a boy? No human has ever touched me. And I am not an outlaw/unchaste person."

The messenger said: "Thus will it be! Your Rabb said: 'It is easy for me to bestow a child without a father. And We will make him an evidence/a sign and a mercy to the people from Us.' And thus it was a matter decreed."

(definition of '*RABB*' in Arabic is '*GOD*')

Well, one of the objectives of this book is to *challenge dogmas and to demystify religious mysteries.*

As evidence, please check for yourselves the evolution of the teachings of the Church since the *Council of Florence, in 1439, to today*; following are limited examples of agreements hammered out at that Council on *limbo, everlasting fire (hell), purgatory, the primacy of the Pope, limitation of salvation to the 'baptised'* and other matters:

'The best unbaptized infants can hope for, according to Catholic theology, is limbo (i.e. a level of hell with no physical sufferings, only the absence of God).

The souls of those who depart this life in actual mortal sin, or in original sin alone, go down straight away to hell to be punished, but with unequal pains (Session 6 — July 6, 1439).

Those who have done good shall go into eternal life, but those who have done evil shall go into eternal fire (Session 8 — Nov. 22, 1439).

[The holy Roman church] firmly believes, professes, and preaches that all those who are outside the Catholic Church, not only pagans but also Jews or heretics and schismatics, cannot share in eternal life

and will go into the everlasting fire which was prepared for the devil and his angels, unless they are joined to the Catholic Church before the end of their lives; that the unity of the ecclesiastical body is of such importance that only for those who abide in it do the Church's sacraments contribute to salvation and do fasts, almsgiving and other works of piety and practices of the Christian militia produce eternal rewards; and that nobody can be saved, no matter how much he has given away in alms and even if he has shed his blood in the name of Christ, unless he has persevered in the bosom and the unity of the Catholic Church (Session 11 — Feb. 4, 1442).

Purgatory as dogma in the Catholic Church... If truly penitent people die in the love of God before they have made satisfaction for acts and omissions by worthy fruits of repentance, their souls are cleansed after death by cleansing pains; and the suffrages of the living faithful avail them in giving relief from such pains, that is, sacrifices of masses, prayers, almsgiving and other acts of devotion which have been customarily performed by some of the faithful for others of the faithful in accordance with the church's ordinances.

We likewise define that the holy, apostolic see and the Roman pontiff hold the primacy over the whole world, and that the Roman pontiff himself is the successor of blessed Peter, prince of the Apostles, and that he is the true vicar of Christ, head of the whole Church and father and teacher of all Christians, and that to the same in blessed Peter was given the full power of feeding, ruling, and governing the whole Church, as is contained also in the acts of the ecumenical councils and the sacred canons"

It was already established that *the 'interpretations' of any religion cannot be stagnant or static*; for Christians, Jesus had confirmed it already, as per the former chapter, according to John 16, 12-13:

'I have MUCH MORE to say to you, more than you can now bear. But when he, the Spirit of truth, comes, he will guide you into ALL the truth. He will not speak on his own; he will speak only what he hears, and he will tell you what is YET TO COME.'

Accordingly, *the Gospel evolves in its 'interpretations'* and *cannot be handcuffed* — so to speak — *by irrefutable, permanent dogmas*.

Allow me to start with the dogma of the *Immaculate Conception*, as per Wikipedia:

'The Immaculate Conception is the belief that the Virgin Mary was free of original sin from the moment of her conception. First debated by medieval theologians, it proved so controversial that it did not become part of official Catholic teaching until 1854, when Pius IX gave it the status of dogma in the papal bull Ineffabilis Deus.'

Well, no one doubts or questions that:

Our Holy Mother was *'born without sin,'*

She is *'full of grace,'*

She is *'blessed among women'* and

She was *sinless during her entire life'*.

However, the dogma refers to the '*original sin*' and that is where I second the '*medieval theologians*' and others who *question the very validity of the 'inheritance' by 'every newborn' of Adam & Eve's sin!*

It is obvious that the story of Adam & Eve in the garden of Eden is only *symbolic*. In fact, both the Bible and Coran confirm this symbolism:

'*Fathers shall not be put to death because of their children, nor shall children be put to death because of their fathers. Each one shall be put to death for his own sin.'* (Deuteronomy 24:16)

'... *No person earns any (sin) except against himself (only), and no bearer of burdens shall bear the burden of another. Then unto your Lord is your return, so He will tell you that wherein you have been differing.'* (Coran 6:164)

Many theologians keep referring to a text by *Saint-Augustin*, relative to the abuse in the *literal understanding of Genesis*; this reference applies to every single *literal interpretation of scriptures* in general; following is the text:

'*8. 37. In matters that are obscure and far beyond our vision, even in such as we may find treated in Holy Scripture, 'different Interpretations' are sometimes possible without prejudice to the faith we have received...*

Now, it is a disgraceful and dangerous thing for an infidel to hear a Christian, presumably giving the meaning of Holy Scripture, talking non-sense on these topics; and we should take all means to prevent such an embarrassing situation, in which people show up vast ignorance in a Christian and laugh it to scorn ...

If they find a Christian mistaken in a field which they themselves know well and hear him maintaining his foolish opinions about our books, how are they going to believe those books in matters concerning the resurrection of the dead, the hope of eternal life, and the kingdom of heaven, when they think their pages are full of <u>falsehoods on facts</u> which they themselves have learnt from experience and the light of reason? Reckless and incompetent expounders of holy Scripture bring untold trouble and sorrow on their wiser brethren when they are caught in one of their mischievous false opinions and are taken to task by those who are not bound by the authority of our sacred books. For then, to defend their utterly foolish and obviously untrue statements, they will try to call upon Holy Scripture for proof and even recite from memory many passages which they think support their position, although "they understand neither what they say nor the things about which they make assertion." (1 Tm 1, 7)

(From: <u>St. Augustine, The Literal Meaning of Genesis</u>, "Ancient Christian Writers," vol. 41. Translated and annotated by John Hammond Taylor, S.J. (New York: Paulist Press, 1982). Retrieved from http://inters.org/augustine-interpretating-sacred-scripture).

I am in full agreement with those two quotations; *<u>I cannot conceive the possible culpability of each and every innocent newborn;</u>* however, this obviously *<u>includes our Mother Mary, at her conception</u> by Saint Anne.*

71

I therefore reiterate that our _Mother Mary was born 'immaculate',_ _just like 'every single newborn,'_ and I deplore two related teachings of the Catholic Church, namely:

the inheritance of an _original sin_ by each and every newborn;

the fact that _dogmas are irrefutable and permanent_;

that a dogma could lead to another, as described below:

My same objection to dogmas also applies to that of _Mary's Assumption_, declared by the 'same' _Pope Pius_ in _1950_, as follows:

'We proclaim and define it to be a dogma revealed by God that the immaculate Mother of God, Mary ever virgin, when the course of her earthly life was finished, was _taken up body and soul into the glory of heaven_.

The declaration was '_built upon_' the 1854 dogma of the Immaculate Conception of Mary, which declared that Mary was _conceived free from_ original sin, and both have their foundation in the concept of Mary as the Mother of God. It leaves open the question of whether Mary _died_ or whether she was raised to eternal life _without bodily death_; the Catholic Church has _two different traditions_ concerning the _assumption/dormition of Mary_: in the first, _she rose from the dead after a brief period_ and _then ascended into heaven_; in the second, she was _"assumed" bodily into heaven before she died_.'

With all due respect to our Blessed Mother, I question both traditions which confirm my _questioning of dogmas_ in the first place; when there is '_doubt,_' _no permanence and irrefutability_ should be allowed. This also applies to the *inheritance of an 'original sin'* by each and every newborn!

I believe that the references to *Mary's Assumption 'prefigure'* the status of humans, *dead and alive,* at the *end of times (Apocalypse)* whereby *all the members of the Body of Christ — Christians and non Christians, believers, atheists and agnostics, alike* — will *resurrect*, thanks to His death and resurrection, as per the Apostles Creed, as follows:

'... the Communion of Saints, the forgiveness of sins, the Resurrection of the body and life everlasting.'

Accordingly, our Blessed Mary resurrected into Heaven, just like we all shall be, *not because of our works*, but *thanks to God's unlimited Mercy*, as explained earlier. However, *with all due respect to our Blessed Mother*, allow me to offer one clarification, as follows:

The Assumption dogma seems to refer to her *human body* rather than to her *mystical* or *transfigured body, as with Christ's transfigured body*, referred to earlier; I tend to doubt this assumption.

Following is a translation of a text from *Father Robert Witwicky*'s book, titled: *'Mary, Questions & Answers:*

'5.1. Did Mary truly ascend to Heaven?

...Pope Pius XII, on November 1, 1960, declared as a dogma that the Virgin Mary, the Immaculate Mother of God, at the end of her life on earth, ascended, soul and body, to eternal glory. Mary is thereby totally immersed in God's love, body and soul, eternally. She is, as declared by Saint Paul, in Col. 3,3:

For you died, and your life is hidden with Christ in God.

The dogmatic formula does not indicate how this has taken place. However, tradition had imagined the occurrence in different ways; some, not numerous, believe that Mary was glorified without dying, just like Christ was transfigured on the Mount, in the presence of His Apostles (Mark 9:2-8), and that she was transported, alive to heaven. For others, Mary ascended at the very instant of her death. Most Christians from the earliest centuries believe in the apocryphal writings that Mary was glorified after her death. Egyptian Christians commemorate, August 22, the opening of Mary's tomb, confirming her Assumption. The passage of Mary from her life on earth to her glorious life in heaven is referred to as her transitus or dormition. Those who hold that belief relate it to that of Christ. They believe that Mary died, but shortly after (three days in Christ's case) was awakened and rose to God's glory. Accordingly, Mary's body was not subjected to corruption in the tomb.'

I second that last point of view in that Mary's *mystic, transfigured body resurrected to heaven*; not her *mortal, earthly, physical body*!

I therefore deplore, one more time, the *dogmatism*, imposed by the Church's *traditions*: both its *permanence* and its *irreversibility*, particularly in this non-factual relevance and its lack of precision, allowing the door to be wide-open to multiple interpretations and queries.

To conclude, *dogmas should be questioned* and *mysteries explained*.

In that particular case of the *Assumption of Mary*, I believe that *Mary's mystical, transfigured body ascended into heaven, just like*

Jesus' body following His resurrection, and as described earlier at His *Transfiguration on the Mount*.

EPILOGUE

Thank you Lord for having allowed me *to express myself so freely,* while having a *clear conscience,* despite my *questioning the irrevocability of the Church's dogmas, the maintenance of mysteries – as such - and certain Church teachings,* and while declaring that our *souls represent 'You' in everyone of our souls, from the very instant of our conception to that of our death; this article of my faith, I truly believe is inspired by the Holy Spirit, and I stand by it.*

I also thank You, Lord God, for having allowed me *to console and liberate my conscience from its constant culpability,* every time *doubts* emerged, relative to my faith, and *questions arose* with every issue I faced in reading the *Bible – particularly with respect to many interpretations of stories from the Old Testament - and also* in examining certain teachings of the Church.

GRANT ME FAITH, LORD, AND FORGIVE MY FAILURES! THANKS A MILLION!

ACKNOWLEDGEMENTS.

Thank you wholeheartedly for your contributions to this book; among many others, to:

- United Church of God, France 'Seven Scientific Proofs of God', Mario Seiglie; *www.ucg.org*)
  7 chemin de Monfaucon – Lot 21
  33127 Martignas sur Jalle
  France

- Brother Robert Witwicki, s.m. (Marianist, Bordeaux).

BOOKS FROM THE SAME AUTHOR :

A) BOOKS PUBLISHED :

- **ANGES TERRESTRES, Nos enfants handicapés,** ISBN, paperback: 978-2-89363-58-4.

- **JE TE DEMANDE PARDON,** ISBN, paperback: 978-2-414180-12-7, ISBN, e-book: 978-2-414180-13-4.

- **SLAVERY OF THE PROVIDER,** ISBN, paperback: 978-2-414174-84-3, ISBN, download: 978-2-414174-85-0.

- **BABY DREAMS & INTELLECT,** ISBN, paperback: 978-2-414159-03-1, ISBN, download: 978-2-414159-04-8.

- **WE ARE ALL MAD,** ISBN, paperback: 978-2-414135-79-0, ISBN, download: 978-2-414135-80-6.

- <u>MY SHADOW & ME,</u>
  ISBN, paperback: 978-2-41417-994-7,
  ISBN, download: 978-2-414179-995-4.

- <u>AGE REVERSAL, TRIUMPHANT FOUNTAIN OF YOUTH,</u>
  ISBN, paperback: 978-2-414155-13-2,
  ISBN, e-book: 978-2-414155-14-9.

- <u>INTELLIGENT, LOGICAL OR WISE, WHO WOULD YOU RATHER BE?</u>
  ISBN, paperback: 978-2-414162-15-4,
  ISBN, e-book: 978-2-414162-16-1.

- <u>THE INVISIBLE ME,</u>
  ISBN, paperback: 978-2-41415-897-2,
  ISBN, e-book: 978-2-41415-898-0.

- <u>A SOUND MIND IN AN UNSOUND BODY,</u>
  ISBN, paperback: 978-2-41415-579-8,
  ISBN, e-book: 978-2-41415-580-4.

- <u>OUR SOUL IS GOD, FROM HIM & TO HIM,</u>
  ISBN, paperback: 978-2-414135-01-4,
  ISBN, e-book: 978-2-41413-501-1.

- <u>BÉBÉS, RÊVES & INTELLIGENCE,</u>
  ISBN, paperback: 978-2-414131-68-6,
  ISBN, e-book: 978-2-414131-69-3.

- <u>FROM WOMB TO TOMB,</u>

ISBN, paperback: 978-2-414131-71-6,
ISBN, e-book: 978-2-4141311-72-3.

- **DE L'ENFER AU PARADIS, DEUX VIES EN UNE,**
  ISBN, paperback: 978-2-414110-59-9,
  ISBN, e-book: 978-2-41411-060-5.

- **LE DOUTE EST UNE CERTITUDE,**
  ISBN, paperback: 978-2-414262-56-4.
  ISBN, e-book: 978-241-4262-57-1.

- **PRIORITIES & POSTERIORITIES,**
  ISBN, paperback: 978-2-414207-57-2,
  ISBN, e-book: 978-2-414207-58-9.

- **I AM 'CAUSE YOU ARE,**
  ISBN, paperback: 978-2-414270-88-0,
  ISBN, e-book: 978-2-414270-89-7.

- **HUMANISM & RELIGIOSITY,**
  ISBN, paperback: 978-2-414262-53-3,
  ISBN, e-book: 978-2-414262-54-0.

- **LOVE YOURSELF FIRST,**
  ISBN, paperback: 978-2-414265-02-2,
  ISBN, download : 978-2-414265-03-9.

- **ALL MEN CREATED EQUAL, TRUE OR FALSE?**
  ISBN, paperback: 978-2-414276967,
  ISBN, e-book: 978-2-414276-97-4.

- **MAY GOD GO BEYOND THE GOSPEL?**

ISBN, paperback: 978-2-414270-79-8,
ISBN, e-book: 978-2-414270-80-4.

- #METOO, COLLATERAL DAMAGES,
ISBN, paperback: 978-2-414226-39-9,
ISBN, e-book: 978-2-414226-40-5.

- VOLUNTEERING IS PRAYING A HUNDREDFOLD,
ISBN, paperback: 978-2-414241-97-2,
ISBN, e-book: 978-2-414241-98-9.

- IF I AM NOT ME, THEN WHOM AM I?
ISBN, paperback: 978-2-414240-14-2,
ISBN, e-book: 978-2-414240-13-5.

- HUSBAND, WIFE OR COMPANION, WHO & HOW TO BEST CHOOSE?
ISBN, paperback: 978-2-414262-50-2,
ISBN, e-book: 978-2-414282-51-9.

- ANGELS & DEMONS, WHO ARE WE?
ISBN, paperback: 978-2-414286-25-6,
ISBN, e-book: 978-2-41428-62-6.

- TAKEN FOR GRANTED,
ISBN, paperback: 978-2-414367-94-8,
ISBN, pdf: 978-2-414367-95-5,
ISBN, epub: 978-2-414367-96-2.

B) *BOOKS NOT YET PUBLISHED :*

1. *Prophetic Utopia*
   (Copyright USA, Registration No. SRU000412448)

2. *Universal Religion*
   (Copyright USA, Registration No. TXU002242048)

3. *Virgin at Age Sixty, Still Yearning*
   (Copyright USA, Registration No. TXU002242048)

4. *Vierge, soixante ans qui se languit d'amour*
   (Copyright USA, Registration No. TXU002242048)

5. *Âme = Dieu, de Lui et À Lui*
   (Copyright USA, Registration No. TXU002242048)

6. *Compulsion vs. Compassion*
   (Copyright USA, Registration No. TXU002242048)

7. *Youth, How to Rekindle their Faith?*
   (Copyright USA, Registration No. TXU002242048)

8. *Jeunes gens, comment rallumer leur foi?*
   (Copyright USA, Registration No. TXU002242048)

9. **Q. & A., Grandkids / Grandpa, Dialogue on a number of issues.**

10. *Divinité & Humanité, Une seule entité, selon la Bible, les Saints, d'autres religions & des notables!*